Who this book is for.

This book is for those who want to learn the basic concepts in C. Many computer science schools have C language in their syllabus in the first year of the study. Now-a-days even schools have included C language in their syllabus.

C is very popular and widely used language across the world. Many languages have been inspired by C. So learning a C will be a first milestone in someone's career. I hope You will enjoy reading this book.

What is covered in this book?

Below concepts are covered in this book.

1. Background of C.
2. Variables and Data Types in C.
3. Executing the C program.
4. Control Statements in C.
5. Arrays in C.
6. Strings in C.
7. Structures and Unions in C.
8. Functions in C.
9. File Handling in C.
10. Memory Management in C
11. Command line arguments
12. Recursion

Table of Contents

1. C Introduction

1.1 C Background

C is a popular computer programing language developed by Dennis Ritchie in 1973 at AT&T Bell Labs.

Main features of C language are.

1. It is a Procedural (Imperative) language.
2. Cross platform programming language.
3. ANSI published the standard for C in 1989 called as C89 and later in 1999 called as C99.
4. Latest ANSI standard for C as of 2014 is C11.
5. C is used in system programming to develop OS.
6. C is also used in embedded systems.
7. C inspired many languages like C++, Java, C#, Perl, Python, PHP etc.
8. C does not have any object oriented features.

1.2 Installation of C compilers and IDE

You can install any of the below mentioned Compiler/IDE for C language.

1. Microsoft Visual C++ 2010 express
2. Microsoft Visual C++ 6.0
3. Turbo C
4. GNU GCC for windows (http://www.mingw.org/)
5. GCC for linux

In this book, most of the examples have been compiled using GCC for windows.

2. Basics of C

2.1 First Program in C

Best way to learn any language is by examples. So let us start with the coding. In this section, we will write a simple C program. File name – abc.c

```c
//include header files
#include<stdio.h>


//main function
void main()
{

    //declare the variables
    int no;
    char a[30];


//clear the screen
system("cls");

//printf function is used to print the
string.

    printf("enter number : ");

//scanf function is used to accept the
input from the user.
    scanf("%d",&no);

    printf("enter string : ");
    scanf("%s",a);

    printf("Display \n");
```

```
    printf("number is : %d \n",no);
    printf("String is : %s ",a);
    getchar();
}
```

Output of the above program is given below.

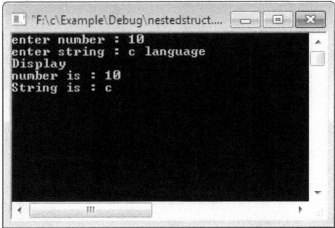

2.2 Explanation

Let us try to understand above program.

Program starts with below lines.

```
//include header files
```

Any line that starts with // is a comment in C. This is used for single line comment. But if you want to comment multiple lines, you can use below syntax.

/*

Comment Line 1

Comment line 2

....so on

*/

Next line starts with #include.

#include is called as a pre-processor directive that can be used to include the contents of header file in the program. We have included 1 header file.

```
#include <stdio.h>
```

<stdio.h> header file contains declarations for functions like prinf, scanf.

Next line starts with void main() function. Every c program has a main function which is the entry point for the program.

In next line, we have declared 2 variables **no** and **a**. Variables are used to store the information. Each variable has a data type.

For example data type of **no** is int. That means this variable can store only integer variables. We will look into more details about variables later in the book.

```
int no;
char a[30];
```

Next line clears the output screen.

```
system("cls");
```

Next lines use printf and scanf functions that can be used to print the output to the console and read data from the user respectively.

Program ends with getchar() function which waits until user enters any character.

In next section, we will see how to compile and execute this program.

2.3 C Basic Syntax.

printf() and scanf() functions are in-built library functions in C which are available in C library by default. These functions are declared and related macros are defined in "stdio.h" which is a header file.

printf() function is used to print the "character, string, float, integer, octal and hexadecimal values" onto the output screen. We use printf() function with below formats

1. %d :- specifier to display the value of an integer variable.
2. %c :- Used to display character,
3. %f :- Used to display float variable.
4. %s :- Used to display string variable.
5. %lf :- Used to display double variable.
6. %x :- Used to display hexadecimal variable.

scanf() function is used to read character, string, numeric data from keyboard.

Please remember below points about C programs.

1. Each statement should end with semicolon.
2. C Program source file has an extension .c
3. We can use {} braces to group the statements in C.

2.4 Compiling and Executing C programs

Compilation and linking of the c program involves below steps.

1. Pre processing – Macro substitution, including of header files.
2. Compilation – generated assembler code
3. Assembly – creates object file
4. Linking – creates executable file by linking library code.

2.4.1 Turbo C compiler

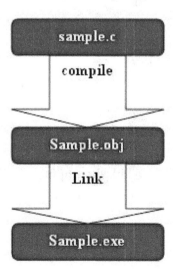

Figure 1-Compiling and Executing the program in turbo C

We can compile c programs using turbo c compiler or Microsoft visual C++.

To compile, build and execute C program in Turbo, you can press ctrl+F9 key combination.

To compile, build and execute C program in Visual C++, you can press ctrl+F5 key combination.

Below image shows how turbo IDE looks like.

Typical phases of C program execution are given in below diagram. The sample.c file contains the source code. After compiling the sample.c, new file is created called sample.obj. This is a intermediate machine code generated by compiler. This is also called as an object file. After compiling the c file, we link the obj file and final exe file is created which can be used to execute the c program.

2.4.2 GCC compiler in windows.

To compile the program using GCC compiler, use below command from command prompt in windows.

11

➢ Gcc abc.c

After compiling the program, a.exe file is created which can be used to execute the c program.

➢ a

2.5 Debugging

Debugging is used to traverse through the program statements one by one. We can watch the variables in the program and find out the reason why code is not working as expected.

Below image shows the Microsoft visual C++ IDE.

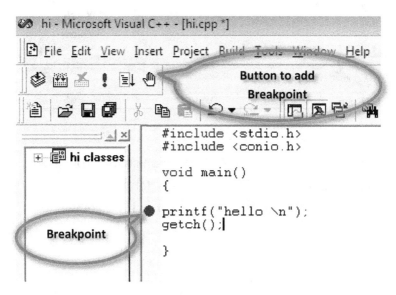

In different IDE, you will see different tools/keystrokes to add/remove breakpoint, step into the function, step out of the function.

You can watch the variables at runtime as well when you are in debug mode as shown in below image.

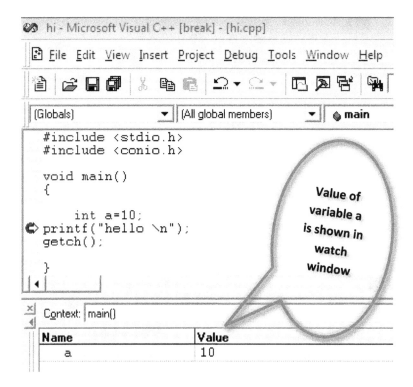

Different IDE provide different mechanism of debugging c program. In Eclipse IDE, you can also debug the programs but the GUI will be different from other IDEs like windows C++ IDE.

2.6 C standard library

Standard library of C is stored in the form of 29 header files as of 2014.

1. <stdio.h>
2. <stdlib.h>

3. <assert.h>
4. <ctype.h>
5. <errno.h>
6. <float.h>
7. <limits.h>
8. <locale.h>
9. <math.h>
10. <setjmp.h>
11. <signal.h>
12. <stdarg.h>
13. <stddef.h>
14. <string.h>
15. <threads.h>
16. <time.h>
17. <iso646.h>
18. <wchar.h>
19. <wctype.h>

C99 standard added below 6 header files.

1. <complex.h>
2. <fenv.h>
3. <inttypes.h>
4. <stdbool.h>
5. <stdint.h>
6. <tgmath.h>

C11 standard added below 5 header files.

1. <stdalign.h>
2. <stdatomic.h>
3. <stdnoreturn.h>
4. <threads.h>

5. <uchar.h>

All header files mentioned above are built-in header files. But we can generate user defined header files as well in C. Please note that each header file contains declarations for important functions.

For example –

<string.h> contains declarations for many string related functions like strlen, strcat, strcpy etc.

3. Data Types and Variables

3.1 Keywords

Below is the list of keywords that are used in C language.
Each keyword has a special meaning.

auto	break	case	char
const	continue	default	do
double	else	enum	extern
float	for	goto	if
int	long	register	return
short	signed	sizeof	static
struct	switch	typedef	union
unsigned	void	volatile	while

3.2 Data Types

Data types are used to specify the how much memory size
will be used to store the data in a variable.

For example –

```
int id;
```
Above statement declares variable Id with data type of int.
int is a data type which needs 2 bytes.

3.2.1 Built in Data types in C.

Data types are used to specify what kind of data a variable
can hold.

Below is the list of Data types in C.

1. char – used to store single character
2. int – used to store natural integer
3. float – used to store single precision numbers
4. double - used to store double precision numbers

We can also use below qualifiers.

1. short – used to store small integer (up to 2 bytes)
2. long – used to store bigger integers (up to 4 bytes)
3. signed – used to store signed numbers.
4. unsigned – used to store unsigned numbers.

To find the size of each data type in terms of bytes, we can use below code. Please note that different machines will produce different outputs based upon processor architecture.

On my 32-bit machine, I got below output.

printf("size of short int is %d", sizeof(short int));

output – 2

printf("size of long int is %d", sizeof(long int));

output – 4

Size of float and double data type is 4 and 8 bytes on my machine respectively.

3.2.2 User defined data types
User defined data types are created using built in data types.

For example, I can define my own data type MYINT which is similar as int.

```c
#include<stdio.h>
int main()
{
    typedef int MYINT;
    MYINT marks=10;
    printf("%d marks", marks);
    getchar();
}
```

```
C:\Users\sagar>gcc point.c

C:\Users\sagar>a
10 marks
```

Above example does not make much sense. But typedef can be very useful when working with structures (We will study structures in detail later on in the book). In below example, we have defined new data type book of type struct book.

```c
#include<stdio.h>
int main()
{

typedef struct
{
int pages;
char * author;
}book;

    book b1;
```

```
    b1.pages = 11;
    printf("%d pages", b1.pages);
    getchar();
}
```

```
C:\Users\sagar>gcc source.c

C:\Users\sagar>a
11 pages
```

3.2.3 Type Conversion in C.

There are two types of data type conversions.

1. Implicit (Automatic type conversion)
2. Explicit (casting)

Sometimes data is lost when compiler does implicit data type conversion. To avoid data loss, we can use explicit type conversion.

Example –

```
#include <stdio.h>

void main()
{
    int marks, subjects;
    double percentage;
    marks = 555;
    subjects = 6;

    //in below statement result will be 92.0
    //percentage= marks / subjects;
```

```
    //in below statement result will
be 92.5 due to explicit type
casting
    percentage=  (double) marks /
subjects;

    printf("Percentage : %f\n",
percentage);

}
```

```
C:\Users\sagar>gcc source.c

C:\Users\sagar>a
Percentage : 92.500000
```

3.3 Variables

Variable is used to store the values. Variables can be declared to be of any data type.

For example –

```
int a;
float b;
```

here a is a variable that can store integer values. b is a variable that can store floating numbers.

Can you guess the output of below c program? In below program, we have declared variable a with int data type. In next statement, we are trying to store 2.2 into a. If you compile this program, you will not see any compilation errors. But the output of the program will be 2 since compiler will truncate the number to nearest integer number closer to 0.

```c
#include<stdio.h>

#include<stdlib.h>
//main function
void main()
{
//declaration of variable
    int a;
//initialisation of variable
    a = 2.2;
//or a = 2.7
    printf("%d",a);
    getchar();
}
```

```
C:\Users\sagar>gcc source.c
C:\Users\sagar>a
2
```

Sometimes we want the variable values to not change. For example in mathematics value of pi never changes. We can declare constant variables using below syntax.

`const float pi=3.14;`
Please note that we can not assign any value to pi later in the program since it is a constant variable.

21

Enumerations are also other type of constants in C. enum is a set of integer constants which are given names.

Below example will help you understand enums in a better way.

```
#include<stdio.h>
#include<stdlib.h>

enum week{ sun, mon, tue, wed, thu,
fri, sat};

int main()
{
    enum week dayname;
    dayname=mon;
    printf("%d day", dayname);
    getchar();
}
```

```
C:\Users\sagar>gcc source.c
C:\Users\sagar>a
1 day
```

Some of Character constants are given below.

No.	Characters	Meaning
1	'\''	Single quote
2	'\"'	Double quote
3	'\?'	Question mark
4	'\a'	Audible alert

5	'\\'	Backslash
6	'\0'	Null
7	'\b'	Back space
8	'\f'	Form feed
9	'\n'	New line
10	'\r'	Carriage return
11	'\t'	Horizontal tab
12	'\v'	Vertical Tab

3.4 Operators

There are 5 types of operators in C.

Arithmetic	-, +, %, /, *
logical	||, &&, !
Relational operators	>, < , >=, <=, !=, ==, !
Bitwise	&, |, ^, ~, <<, >>
Assignment	=, +=, -=, *=, /=, %=, &=
increment & decrement operators	++,--
Conditional	?: True or false

4. Control Statements in C

Now let us try to understand the control statements in C Language.

4.1 if...else

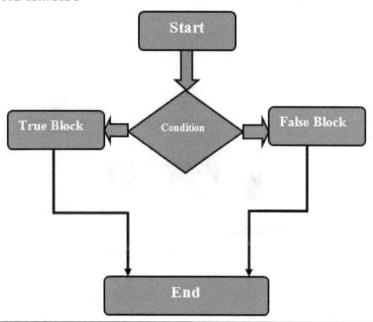

Above diagram illustrates how if else construct works in c language. Condition is tested in if else construct and if that condition turns out to be true, control goes to true block (if block) otherwise it goes to false block (else block).

Program to find whether number is even or odd

```
#include<stdio.h>
void main()
{
  Int n;
  system("cls")
```

```
printf("Enter no");
scanf("%d",&n);
if(n%2==0)
  {
    printf("\n%d is even number",n);
  }
else
  {
    printf("\n%d is odd number",n);
  }
getchar();

}
```

```
Enter no4
4 is even number
```

Program to compare two numbers.

```
#include<stdio.h>

void main()
{
  int a,b;
  printf("\n Enter 1st number : ");
  scanf("%d: ",&a);
  printf("\n Enter 2nd number : ");
  scanf("%d: ",&b);
  if(a>b)
  {
    printf("\n The greater number is a :
%d",a);
  }
  else
  {
    printf("\n The greater number is b :
%d",b);
```

```
    }
    getchar();
}
```

```
C:\Users\sagar>gcc source.c
C:\Users\sagar>a
 Enter 1st number : 12
 Enter 2nd number : 34
 The greater number is b : 34
```

Program to check whether Year is leap or not.

```c
#include<stdio.h>

void main()
{
   int year;
   printf("\n Enter Year : ");
   scanf("%d: ",&year);
   if(year%4==0)
   {
     printf("\n The %d is leap year.
",year);
   }
   else
   {
     printf("\n The %d is not leap
year.",year);
   }
   getchar();
}
```

```
C:\Users\sagar>gcc source.c

C:\Users\sagar>a

Enter Year : 2014

The 2014 is not leap year.
```

Program to accept character from user and check whether it is vowel or consonant .

```c
#include<stdio.h>

void main()
{
  char ch;
  printf("\n Enter character : ");
  scanf("%c: ",&ch);

if(ch=='a'||ch=='e'||ch=='i'||ch=='o'||ch=='u')
  {
    printf("\n The %c is vowel. ",ch);
  }
  else
  {
    printf("\n The %c is consonant.",ch);
  }
  getchar();
}
```

```
C:\Users\sagar>gcc source.c

C:\Users\sagar>a

Enter character : d

The d is consonant.
```

4.2 Switch statement

Switch case statements are used in scenarios where there are multiple flows depending upon the condition.

Depending upon the switch expression, specific case block is executed. Switch expression is evaluated as a constant value.

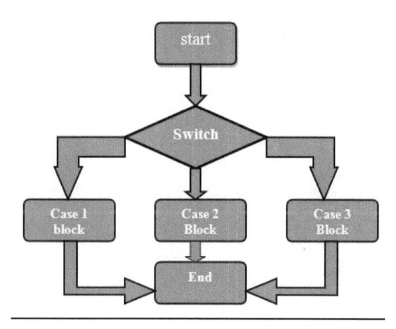

Below program demonstrates the use of switch statement in C.

```
#include<stdio.h>
void main()
{
    int n;
```

```
  printf("Enter choice");
  scanf("%d",&n);

  switch (n)
  {
    case 1:
          printf("One");
          break;
    case 2:
          printf ("Two");
          break;
    case 3:
          printf ("Three");
          break;
    case 4:
          printf ("Four");
          break;
    case 5:
          printf ("Five");
          break;
    default:
          printf ("invalid value ");
          break;
  }
  getchar();

}
```

```
C:\Users\sagar>gcc source.c

C:\Users\sagar>a
Enter choice4
Four
```

4.3 While Loop

Program 1: Print 1 to 10 numbers.

```
#include<stdio.h>
```

```
void main()
{
  int n=1;
  while(n<=10)
    {
      printf("\n %d",n);
      n++;
    }
  getchar();
}
```

Program 2 : Write a program to find out factorial of a number.

```
#include<stdio.h>

void main()
{
  int no,fact=1,i=1;
  system("cls");
  printf("\n Enter the number: ");
  scanf("%d",&no);
  while(i<=no)
  {
    fact=fact*i;
    i++;
  }
```

```
    printf("\n Factorial of a number is :
%d",fact);

getchar();
}
```

```
Enter the number: 5
Factorial of a number is : 120
```

Program 3 : Find whether number is prime or not .

```c
#include<stdio.h>

void main()
{
   int no;
   system("cls");
   printf("\n Enter the number: ");
   scanf("%d",&no);
   if(no==1||no==2||no==3||no==5||no==7)
   {
     printf("\n %d is prime number",no);
   }
   else  if(no%2>0 && no%3>0 && no%5>0 &&
no%7>0)
   {
     printf("\n %d is prime number",no);
   }
   else
   {
     printf("\n %d is not prime",no);
   }
getchar();
}
```

```
Enter the number: 7

7 is prime number
```

Program 4: Write a program count the number of digit in the number .

```c
#include<stdio.h>

void main()
{
   int no,r=0,count=0;
   system("cls");
   printf("\n Enter the number: ");
   scanf("%d",&no);
   while(no!=0)
   {
      r=no%10;
      count++;
      no=no/10;
   }
   printf("\n The number of digits are
%d",count);

getchar();
}
```

```
Enter the number: 345

The number of digits are 3
```

Program 5 : Write a program to sum of digit the number.

```c
#include<stdio.h>

void main()
{
```

```c
   int no,r=0,sum=0;
   system("cls");
   printf("\n Enter the number: ");
   scanf("%d",&no);
   while(no!=0)
   {
      r=no%10;
      sum=sum+r;
      no=no/10;
   }
   printf("\n The number of digits are
%d",sum);

getchar();
}
```

```
Enter the number: 567
The number of digits are 18
```

Program 6 : Print 1 to 10 Fibonacci series .

```c
#include<stdio.h>

void main()
{
   int i=1;
   int no1=0,no2=1,fib=0;
   system("cls");
   while(i<=10)
   {
      fib=no1+no2;
      printf("\t %d",fib);
      no1=no2;
      no2=fib;
      i++;
   }
```

```
getchar();
}
```

Program 7 : Check whether number is Armstrong or not .

```
#include<stdio.h>

void main()
{
   int no,r=0,sum=0;

   system("cls");
   printf("\n Enter the number : ");
   scanf("%d",&no);
   int temp=no;
   while(no!=0)
   {
      r=no%10;
      sum=sum+(r*r*r);
      no=no/10;
   }

   if(temp==sum)
   {
       printf("%d is Armstrong
number",temp);
   }
   else
```

```
   {
     printf("%d is not Armstrong
number",temp);
   }

   getchar();

}
```

```
Enter the number : 345
345 is not Armstrong number
```

4.4 Do ...While Loop

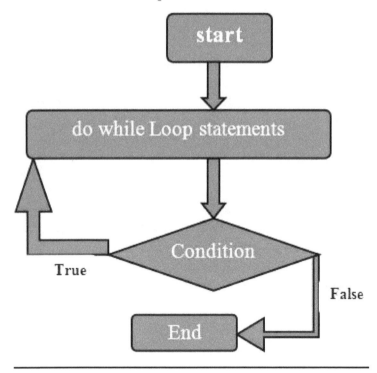

Program 1 : Print 1 to 10 numbers using do while.

```
#include<stdio.h>
```

```
void main()
{
  int a=1;
  system("cls");
  do
   {
     printf("\n%d",a);
     a++;
   }while(a<=10);
 getchar();
}
```

Program 2 : Print only multiple of 5 using do while from 1 to 50 numbers .

```
#include<stdio.h>

void main()
{
  int i=1;
  do
  {
    if(i%5==0)
     {
       printf("\n %d",i);
     }
    i++;
  }while(i<=50);

  getchar();
}
```

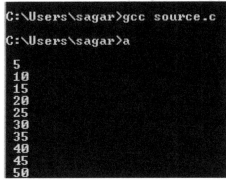

4.4 for Loop

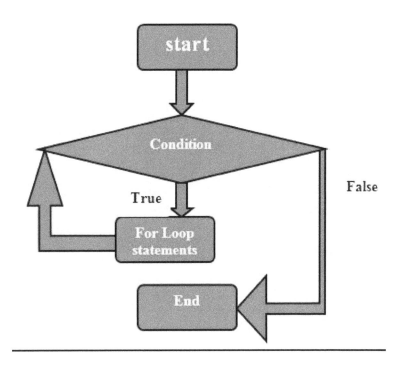

Program to display Addition of 1 to 50 numbers .

```
#include<stdio.h>

void main()
```

37

```
{
  int i=1,sum=0;
  for(i=1;i<=50;i++)
  {
    sum=sum+i;
  }
  printf("\n sum of 1 to 50 numbers is :
%d",sum);

  getchar();
}
```

```
C:\Users\sagar>gcc source.c
C:\Users\sagar>a
 sum of 1 to 50 numbers is : 1275
```

Program to accept 20 numbers from the user & count the number of positive values,negative values & zeros.

```
#include<stdio.h>

void main()
{
  int i=1,no,z=0,p=0,n=0;
  for(i=1;i<=20;i++)
  {
      printf("\n Enter values:");
      scanf("%d",&no);
      if(no==0)
      {
         z++;
      }
      if(no>0)
      {
         p++;
      }
```

```
        if(no<0)
        {
          n++;
        }

  }
  printf("\n Zeros no is :%d",z);
  printf("\n Positive no is :%d",p);
  printf("\n Negative no is :%d",n);

  getchar();
}
```

```
Enter values:3

Enter values:-2

Enter values:4

Enter values:-1

Enter values:0

Zeros no is :1
Positive no is :2
Negative no is :2
```

Program to display series of 1 to 15 numbers in reverse order and display the sum of 1 to 15 numbers .

```
#include<stdio.h>

void main()
{
  int i=0,sum=0;
  int fno=15,sno=1;
  for(i=fno;i>=sno;i--)
  {
      printf("%d \t",i);
      sum=sum+i;
```

```
    }
    printf("\n Sum is :%d",sum);

    getchar();
}
```

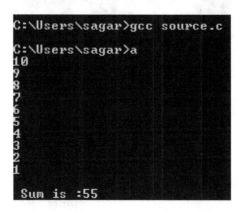

4.5 Break and Continue

In many situations we need to come out of the loop in the middle based upon some conditions.

In C, we can use **break** keyword to come out of loop. After the break statement is executed control goes to the first statement after loop.

```
#include <stdio.h>

void main()
{
int i=0;
while(i<10)
{
    printf("%d",i);
    if (i==5)
```

```
    break;
    i++;
  }
}
```

```
C:\Users\sagar>gcc source.c
C:\Users\sagar>a
012345
```

In above example, we have used break statement to come out of while loop. Above loop will print the values from 0 to 5.

Similarly we have **continue** keyword that can be used to get the control to the beginning of the loop. After continue statement is executed, all the statements after continue are skipped and control goes to the condition statement in the loop.

Example on continue keyword in C.

```
#include <stdio.h>

void main()
{
   int i=0;

   while(i<10)
   {
   i++;
   if (i%2==0)
   continue;
   printf("%d",i);
   }
}
```

```
C:\Users\sagar>gcc source.c
C:\Users\sagar>a
13579
```

In above example we have used **continue** statement to print only odd numbers. If the number is even, control goes to the beginning of the loop.

4.6 goto statement in C.

C provides one keyword goto which can be used to transfer the control to any logical statement. Below program will print "**hello**" twice as we jumped to the label called **jump**. Please note that label name can be any valid name.

```
#include<stdio.h>
#include<stdlib.h>

void main()
{
int i=0;
jump:
printf ("hello");

if (i==0)
{
i++;
goto jump;
}

}
```

```
C:\Users\sagar>gcc source.c

C:\Users\sagar>a
hellohello
```

5. Functions In C

Functions are a block of statements which can be reused.

As shown in below image, each function takes input, does the processing on that input and then produces the output.

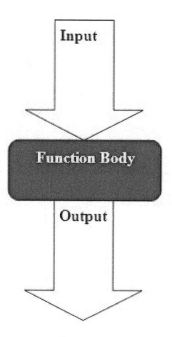

5.1 Uses of C functions

- C functions are used to avoid rewriting same logic/code again and again in a program.
- There is no limit in calling C functions to make use of same functionality wherever required.
- We can call functions any number of times in a program and from any place in a program.
- A large C program can easily be tracked when it is divided into functions.

- The core concept of C functions is re-usability and dividing a big task into small pieces.

5.2 Built in VS user defined

There are 2 types of functions.

1. Built-in functions.
2. User Defined functions.

Built-in functions are defined in the standard c library while user defined functions are created by user.

For example –

printf is a built-in function that can be used to print the data to standard output console.

We will see how to define the user defined functions in next 2 sections.

5.3 Function Declaration

Each function takes input and produces output.

Input can be of any data type.

Example –

```
int sum (int a, int b)
```

In above statement, we have declared function with name sum which takes input in the form of 2 arguments a and b of type int and returns the output in the form of integer type.

5.4 Function definition:

Sample example on function is given below. We have defined one function with name **add**

Add function takes 2 inputs p1 and p2 and returns one variable with int data type.

```c
#include<stdio.h>

int add( int p1,int p2 );

void main()
{
    int a=10;
    int b=20, c;
    //we are calling add function here
    //a and b are actual arguments
    c = add( a, b );
    printf("sum of a and b is %d \n", c);
}

int add( int p1,int p2 )
{
    int t;
    t=p1+p2;
    return t;
}
```

```
C:\Users\sagar>gcc source.c

C:\Users\sagar>a
sum of a and b is 30
```

5.5 Calling a function

We can call function in C in 2 ways.

1. Call by value
2. Call by reference

5.5.1 Call by value

In this method, copies of the actual arguments are passed to the function. Actual arguments will not be modified by called function.

For Example:

```c
#include<stdio.h>
// function prototype, also called
function declaration
void swap(int p, int q);

int main()
{
    int a = 10, b = 20;
    // calling swap function by value
    printf("Before swapping\n a = %d \n
b=%d",a,b);
    swap(a,b);
}

void swap(int p, int q)
{
    int t;
    t = p;
    p = q;
    q = t;
    printf(" \nAfter swapping \n a =
%d\n and b = %d \n", p, q);
}
```

Output:

```
C:\Users\sagar>gcc source.c

C:\Users\sagar>a
Before swapping
 a = 10
 b=20
After swapping
 a = 20
 and b = 10
```

5.5.2 Call by reference (Using pointer)

In this method, addresses of the actual arguments are passed to the function using pointers. Actual arguments may be modified by called function. Memory is saved in this method.

For Example:

```c
#include<stdio.h>
// function prototype, also called
function declaration
void swap(int *p, int *q);

int main()
{

    int a = 17, b = 27;
    // calling swap function by
reference
    printf("Before swapping \n a = %d \n
b = %d",a,b);

//we have passed the addresses of a and
b

    swap(&a, &b);
```

```
     printf("\n After swapping \n a = %d
\n b = %d", a, b);



}

void swap(int *p, int *q)
{
    int t;
    t = *p;
    *p = *q;
    *q = t;
}
```

5.6 Recursions

Mechanism in which a function makes a call to itself is called as recursion.

Sample program to demonstrate recursion.

```
#include <stdio.h>

int getfactorial(int i)
{
    if(i == 1)
    {
        return 1;
    }
    return i * getfactorial(i - 1);
```

```
}

void main()
{
    int i = 4;
    printf("Factorial of %d is %d\n", i,
getfactorial(i));
}
```

```
C:\Users\sagar>gcc source.c

C:\Users\sagar>a
Factorial of 4 is 24
```

5.7 Passing variable number of arguments

Sometimes the input to the function is not fixed. Total number of arguments to the function is not same.

In such scenarios, we can use concept called variable arguments which allows us to define the functions that take variable number of arguments. In below example, we have used sum function which takes different number of arguments and of different types.

Please note that while calling the function, we have used first parameter to specify the total number of arguments to be passed.

```
#include <stdio.h>
#include <stdarg.h>

double sum(int num, ...);
```

```
int main()
{
    printf("Sum of 2.0, 3, 4, 5 = %f\n",
sum(4, 2.0,3,4,5));
    printf("Sum of 5.5, 10, 11,22,15 =
%f\n", sum(5, 5.5,10,11,22,15));
}
double sum(int num,...)
{
    va_list valist;
    double rsum = 0.0;
    int i;
    va_start(valist, num);
    for (i = 0; i < num; i++)
    {
        if (i==0)
                //first argument will be
double type.
            rsum += va_arg(valist,
double);
        else
                //arguments will be int
type except first param.
            rsum += va_arg(valist, int);
    }
//release the memory of valist
    va_end(valist);
    return rsum;
}
```

```
C:\Users\sagar>gcc source.c

C:\Users\sagar>a
Sum of 2.0, 3, 4, 5 = 14.000000
Sum of 5.5, 10, 11,22,15 = 63.500000
```

6. Arrays

6.1 Declaring Arrays

Consider below statement.

```
int marks;
```

In above statement, **marks** is a integer variable which occupies just 2 bytes in the memory. We can store only single value at any point of time.

Arrays can be used to store multiple values. Arrays are used to store multiple values in the contiguous locations in memory.

Sample array representation in memory is given below.

```
int a[6];
```

22	32	1	66	8	12
0	1	2	3	4	5

In above figure, we have an array of size 6. Please note that Array index starts at 0.

So to get the first element in array we have to use below syntax.

X = a[0];

After execution of above statement, Variable X will contain 22.

The above mentioned array is 1-dimensional array.

We can also create multi dimensional arrays.

1. 2-dimensional array
2. 3-dimensional array and so on..

6.2 One dimensional Array

Below program demonstrates how to use 1-dimensional array in C.

```c
#include<stdio.h>


void main()
{
  //Declare and initialize the array
with 5 elements.

  int a[5]={2,4,3,6,10};
  //Please note that we can not store
more than 5 elements in above array.

  int i=0;

  for(i=0;i<=4;i++)          // for loop is
used to iterate through the array from 0
to 4
    {
      printf("\n %d",a[i]);
        // printing value of ith location
of an array
    }

  getchar();
}
```

```
C:\Users\sagar>gcc source.c

C:\Users\sagar>a

2
4
3
6
10
```

Please note that we can store only similar data type values in the array. In above example, we can store only integer values in array a. We can not store floating numbers like 12.4 in above array. To store such number, you will have to declare the array of type float.

Program to Accept 5 element from user & Display sum of elements.

```c
#include<stdio.h>

void main()
{

    int a[5];

    int i=0,sum=0;

    for(i=0;i<=4;i++)
      {
        printf("\n Enter %d position Array
Element :",i);
        scanf("%d",&a[i]);
        sum=sum+a[i];
      }
    printf("\n Sum=%d",sum);

    getchar();
```

```
}
```

```
C:\Users\sagar>gcc source.c

C:\Users\sagar>a

  Enter 0 position Array Element :3

  Enter 1 position Array Element :4

  Enter 2 position Array Element :7

  Enter 3 position Array Element :1

  Enter 4 position Array Element :8

  Sum=23
```

Program to accept integer values in two arrays & sum them into third array.

```c
#include<stdio.h>


void main()
{


   int a[5],b[5],c[5];

   int i=0,sum=0;
   printf("Enter First Array element
\n");
   for(i=0;i<=4;i++)
     {
       printf("\n Enter %d position Array
Element :",i);
       scanf("%d",&a[i]);

     }
```

```
  printf("Enter Second Array element
\n");
  for(i=0;i<=4;i++)
    {
      printf("\n Enter %d position Array
Element :",i);
      scanf("%d",&b[i]);
    }
  printf("Addition stored in third array
\n");
  for(i=0;i<=4;i++)
    {
      c[i]=a[i]+b[i];
      printf(" c[%d]=%d \n",i,c[i]);
    }
getchar();
}
```

```
C:\Users\sagar>gcc source.c

C:\Users\sagar>a
Enter First Array element

  Enter 0 position Array Element :2

  Enter 1 position Array Element :4

  Enter 2 position Array Element :6

  Enter 3 position Array Element :1

  Enter 4 position Array Element :7
Enter Second Array element

  Enter 0 position Array Element :8

  Enter 1 position Array Element :23

  Enter 2 position Array Element :4

  Enter 3 position Array Element :6

  Enter 4 position Array Element :77
Addition stored in third array
  c[0]=10
  c[1]=27
  c[2]=10
  c[3]=7
  c[4]=84
```

Program to sort given Array in Ascending order.

```
#include<stdio.h>


void main()
{
  int a[5];
  int i=0,j=0,temp=0;

  printf("Enter Array element \n");
  for(i=0;i<=4;i++)
  {
    printf("\n Enter %d position Array
Element :",i);
```

```
      scanf("%d",&a[i]);
   }
  for(j=0;j<=4;j++)
  {
    for(i=0;i<=4;i++)
        {
          if(a[i+1]<a[i])
          {
              temp=a[i];
              a[i]=a[i+1];
              a[i+1]=temp;

          }
        }
    }
printf("Array in ascending order
is:\n");
for(i=0;i<=4;i++)
{
      printf("%d\n",a[i]);

}

  getchar();
}
```

```
C:\Users\sagar>gcc source.c

C:\Users\sagar>a
Enter Array element

 Enter 0 position Array Element :4

 Enter 1 position Array Element :5

 Enter 2 position Array Element :7

 Enter 3 position Array Element :2

 Enter 4 position Array Element :9
Array in ascending order is:
2
4
5
7
9
```

6.3 Multidimensional Array

Multi-dimensional arrays can be used in many scenarios like matrix operations.

Program to accept elements for 3 x 3 matrix & display the contents is given below.

```c
#include<stdio.h>


void main()
{
  int a[3][3];
  int r,c;

  printf("Enter Array element \n");

  for(r=0;r<=2;r++)
   {
     for(c=0;c<=2;c++)
      {
```

```
        printf("\n enter a[%d][%d]
:",r,c);
          scanf("%d",&a[r][c]);
      }
   }
 printf("Display Array element \n");

 for(r=0;r<=2;r++)
   {
     for(c=0;c<=2;c++)
       {

printf("a[%d][%d]=%d\n" ,r,c,a[r][c]);


       }
    }
   getchar();
}
```

```
C:\Users\sagar>gcc source.c

C:\Users\sagar>a
Enter Array element

 enter a[0][0] :2

 enter a[0][1] :4

 enter a[0][2] :6

 enter a[1][0] :5

 enter a[1][1] :7

 enter a[1][2] :23

 enter a[2][0] :12

 enter a[2][1] :4

 enter a[2][2] :8
Display Array element
a[0][0]=2
a[0][1]=4
a[0][2]=6
a[1][0]=5
a[1][1]=7
a[1][2]=23
a[2][0]=12
a[2][1]=4
a[2][2]=8
```

Program to add 2 matrices of 3 x 3 dimensions is given below.

```
#include<stdio.h>

void main()
{
   int a[3][3];
   int b[3][3];
   int d[3][3];
     int r,c;
   printf("Enter First Array element
\n");
   for(r=0;r<=2;r++)
```

```
    {
            for(c=0;c<=2;c++)
            {
            printf("\n enter a[%d][%d]
:",r,c);
                scanf("%d",&a[r][c]);
            }
    }

 printf("Enter Second Array element
\n");
   for(r=0;r<=2;r++)
   {
            for(c=0;c<=2;c++)
            {
            printf("\n b[%d][%d] :",r,c);
                scanf("%d",&b[r][c]);
            }
   }
   printf("Addition stored in third array
\n");
   for(r=0;r<=2;r++)
   {
            for(c=0;c<3;c++)
            {
        d[r][c]=a[r][c]+b[r][c];
            printf(" d[%d][%d]=%d
\n",r,c,d[r][c]);
            }
   }

 getchar();
}
```

```
C:\Users\sagar>a
Enter First Array element

enter a[0][0] :3

enter a[0][1] :2

enter a[0][2] :6

enter a[1][0] :5

enter a[1][1] :8

enter a[1][2] :9

enter a[2][0] :45

enter a[2][1] :3

enter a[2][2] :22
Enter Second Array element

b[0][0] :12

b[0][1] :34

b[0][2] :4

b[1][0] :7

b[1][1] :4

b[1][2] :8

b[2][0] :9

b[2][1] :1

b[2][2] :66
Addition stored in third array
d[0][0]=15
d[0][1]=36
d[0][2]=10
d[1][0]=12
d[1][1]=12
d[1][2]=17
d[2][0]=54
d[2][1]=4
d[2][2]=88
```

63

7. String

7.1 Introduction

Strings are nothing but sequence of characters.

We can store the strings in c using character arrays.

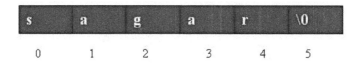

s	a	g	a	r	\0
0	1	2	3	4	5

The last character in the character array is always '\0' (null). It marks the end of the string.

Below are some of the different ways of storing the strings in c.

7.2 Character arrays declaration

Syntax:

```c
char str[number-of-characters];

char str1[] = "sagar";

char str2[3] = {'a','b','\0'};

char str3[6] = "sagar";

char* str4;
```

Declaration of string
    Example 1:
      `char name[15];`

Initializing string

Example 2:
```
char name[15]="Sagar salunke";
```
Below program will calculate the length of the string.

```c
#include<stdio.h>

void main()
{
        char str[15];
        int i=0;
        printf("\n Enter String : ");
        scanf("%s",str);
        while(str[i]!='\0')
        {
                i++;

        }
    printf("\n %s Length is=%d\n",str,i);
    getchar();
}
```

```
C:\Users\sagar>gcc source.c
C:\Users\sagar>a
 Enter String : welcome
 welcome Length is=7
```

Below program will reverse the given string.

```c
#include<stdio.h>

void main()
{
        char str[15];
        int i=0,j=0;
        printf("\n Enter String : ");
```

65

```
          scanf("%s",str);

          printf("\n String is :%s\n",str);
          while(str[i]!=NULL)
          {
                    i++;

          }
          printf("Reverse string is:");

          for(j=i;j>=0;j--)
          {
                    printf("%c",str[j]);
          }
     getchar();
}
```

```
C:\Users\sagar>gcc source.c

C:\Users\sagar>a

 Enter String : welcome

 String is :welcome
Reverse string is: emoclew
```

Below program will count the vowels and consonants in the string.

```
#include<stdio.h>

void main()
{
   char s1[15];
   int i=0,c1=0,c2=0;
   printf("\n Enter first String : ");
   scanf("%s",s1);

   while(s1[i]!='\0')
```

```
    {
       if(s1[i]=='a'||s1[i]=='e'||s1[i]=
='i'||s1[i]=='o'||s1[i]=='u')
       {
         c1++;
       }
       else
       {
         c2++;
       }
       i++;
    }
  printf("\n Entered string is :%s",s1);
printf("\n Number of vowels is :%d",c1);
printf("\n Number of consonants is
:%d",c2);

    getchar();
}
```

```
C:\Users\sagar>gcc source.c

C:\Users\sagar>a

Enter first String : Hello

Entered string is :Hello
Number of vowels is :2
Number of consonants is :3
```

Below program will convert the upper case string to lower case.

```
#include<stdio.h>

void main()
{
  char str[15];
  int i=0;
  printf("\n Enter String : ");
```

```
    scanf("%s",str);

    printf("\n String is :%s\n",str);
    while(str[i]!='\0')
      {
        if(str[i]>=65 && str[i]<=96)
          {
            str[i]=str[i]+32;
          }
          i++;
      }
    printf("Converted string is:%s",str);
    getchar();
}
```

```
C:\Users\sagar>gcc source.c

C:\Users\sagar>a

 Enter String : WELCOME

 String is :WELCOME
Converted string is:welcome
```

Below program will copy one string into another.

```
#include<stdio.h>

void main()
{
   char s1[15],s2[15];
   int i=0;
   printf("\n Enter first String : ");
   scanf("%s",s1);

   printf("\n Enter second String : ");
   scanf("%s",s2);
```

```
   printf("\nBefore copying:");
   printf("\n First string :%s \n Second
string :%s",s1,s2);

   for(i=0;i<=14;i++)
   {
      s2[i]=s1[i];
   }

   printf("\n After copying:");
   printf("\n First string :%s \n Second
string :%s",s1,s2);
   getchar();
}
```

```
C:\Users\sagar>gcc source.c

C:\Users\sagar>a

 Enter first String : welcome

 Enter second String : hello

Before copying:
 First string :welcome
 Second string :hello
After copying:
 First string :welcome
 Second string :welcome
```

7.3 Built-in String Functions

In C there are 6 types of library functions as mentioned below.

String functions

1. strcpy(s1,s2);   //Copies one string(s1) into another string(s1).
2. strcat(s1,s2);   //Concatenates two strings.
3. strlen(s1);   //Returns the length of string.
4. strcmp(s1,s2);   //Compare two strings.

69

5. strchr(s1,ch);
6. strstr(s1,s2);

Below program compares 2 strings

```c
#include<stdio.h>

#include<string.h>

void main()
{
    char str1[15],str2[15];

    printf("Enter the first string\n");
    gets(str1);
    printf("Enter the second string\n");
    gets(str2);
    if( strcmp(str1,str2) == 0 )
      {
        printf("String is equal.\n");
      }

    else if( strcmp(str1,str2)< 0)
      {
        printf("Str1 is less than
str2\n");
      }
    else
      {
        printf("Str1 is greater than
str2\n");
      }
    getchar();
}
```

```
C:\Users\sagar>gcc source.c

C:\Users\sagar>a
Enter the first string
hello
Enter the second string
welcome
Str1 is less than str2
```

Below program concatenates 2 strings.

```
#include<stdio.h>

#include<string.h>
void main()
{
    char str1[10];
    char str2[10];
        //accept the first string
    printf("Enter First string");
    scanf("%s",str1);

        //accept the second string
    printf("Enter second string");
    scanf("%s",str2);

        //concatenate string2 into string1
    strcat( str1, str2);

    printf("Concatenated string is:
%s\n", str1 );

 getchar();

}
```

```
C:\Users\sagar>gcc source.c

C:\Users\sagar>a
Enter First stringgreen
Enter second stringRed
Concatenated string is: greenRed
```

C programming for beginners

Below program will illustrate how we can format the string using printf function.

```c
#include<stdio.h>


void main()
{
   //print whole string
   printf("*%s*\n", "Sagar Salunke");

     //Reserve 50 spaces for printing
string...
        //if string is less than 50, oher
characters will be blank spaces
        //- sign indicates that printing
will be left justified
     printf("*%-50s*\n", "Sagar Salunke");

        //Reserve 50 spaces for printing
string...
        //if string is less than 50, oher
characters will be blank spaces
        //No sign indicates that printing
will be right justified
     printf("*%50s*\n", "Sagar Salunke");

     //print 5 characters from string...
     printf("*%.5s*\n", "Sagar Salunke");

     //print 10 characters from
string...
     printf("*%.10s*\n","Sagar Salunke");

     //Reserve 50 spaces for printing
string...
        //but print only 10 characters
from string...
```

72

```
  printf("*%50.10s*\n","Sagar Salunke");

      //Reserve 50 spaces for printing
string...
      //but print only 10 characters
from string right justified...
    printf("*%-50.10s*\n","Sagar
Salunke");

  getchar();
}
```

```
C:\Users\sagar>gcc source.c

C:\Users\sagar>a
Enter First stringgreen
Enter second stringRed
Concatenated string is: greenRed

C:\Users\sagar>gcc source.c

C:\Users\sagar>a
*Sagar Salunke*
*Sagar Salunke                                      *
*                                       Sagar Salunke*
*Sagar*
*Sagar Salu*
*                                          Sagar Salu*
*Sagar Salu                                          *
```

Below program will append one string to another.

```
#include<stdio.h>
#include<string.h>
void main()

{
char str1[100];
char str2[20];
char str3[30];

int i=0,str1len,str2len;
```

73

```
printf("\nEnter first string -> ");
scanf("%s",str1);
printf("\nEnter second string -> ");
scanf("%s",str2);

//using built in function from string.h
library
printf("\n Concatenated string is
%s",strcat(str1,str2));

//using user defined logic.

//1. find the length of the both strings
and then use for loop.

str1len = strlen(str1);
str2len = strlen(str2);

while(i < str2len)
{
str1[str1len+i] = str2[i];
i++;
}

str1[str1len+i] = '\0';

printf("\nWithout using strcat -> %s",
str1 );


getchar();
}
```

```
C:\Users\sagar>gcc source.c

C:\Users\sagar>a

Enter first string -> sagar

Enter second string -> salunke

 Concatenated string is sagarsalunke
Without using strcat -> sagarsalunkesalunke
```

8. Pointers In C

8.1 Introduction

Pointers are used to hold the addresses of the variables.

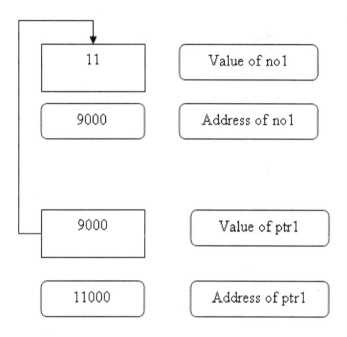

Above diagram illustrates the working of pointers. There is one variable called no1. We have declared pointer ptr1. ptr1 is storing the address of no1.

Declaration of normal variable and pointer variable.

```
int no1=11 ;
int *ptr1;
```

To store the address of variable no1, we have used below syntax.

ptr1 = &no1;

To get the value pointed by ptr1, we can use below syntax.

X = *ptr1;

8.2 Simple pointer Example

```
#include<stdio.h>

void main()
{
    int no=0;
    int *ptr;
    system("cls");
    printf("\n Enter number:");
    scanf("%d",&no);
    ptr=&no;
    printf("\n %d is stored at
%u",no,ptr);
getchar();
}
```

```
Enter number:56
56 is stored at 2293528
```

8.3 Pointers and functions

We can pass arguments by reference using pointers in C. We can also return a pointer from the function.

In below function, we have created one function called swap which takes 2 arguments. We have used pointers to pass the arguments by address.

```
#include<stdio.h>
// function prototype, also called
function declaration
void swap(int *p, int *q);

int main()
{

    int a = 10, b = 20;
    // calling swap function by
reference
    printf("Before swapping \n a = %d \n
b = %d",a,b);
    swap(&a, &b);
    printf("\n After swapping \n a = %d
\n b = %d", a, b);



}

void swap(int *p, int *q)
{
    int t;
    t = *p;
    *p = *q;
    *q = t;
}
```

```
C:\Users\sagar>gcc source.c

C:\Users\sagar>a
Before swapping
 a = 10
  b = 20
 After swapping
 a = 20
 b = 10
```

8.4 Pointers and Arrays.

Arrays are special type of pointer.

When we declare an array, the name of array contains the address of array's first element.

```c
#include <stdio.h>

void squares(int *a, int size)
{
int i;
for (i=0;i<size;i++)
{
*(a+i) = *(a+i) * *(a+i);
}

}

int main()
{
    int myarray[3] = {2,3,4};
    int i;

  //both statements will print same
address value

  printf("myarray contains %u
\n",myarray);
  printf("&myarray contains %u
\n",&myarray);

  squares(myarray,3);

  for(i=0;i<3;i++)
   printf("%d   ", myarray[i]);
}
```

```
C:\Users\sagar>gcc source.c

C:\Users\sagar>a
myarray contains 2293520
&myarray contains 2293520
4    9    16
```

8.5 Pointers and Strings.

Since strings are stored in the form of character arrays, we can use pointers to manipulate the strings.

Below program shows how we can use pointers to handle the strings in C.

```c
#include <stdio.h>
#include <stdlib.h>
void main()
{

        char *s1, *s2, *s3;
        int i=0,j=0;

        //Below statement will reserve 5
bytes and initialize s1 to it
        s1 = "Bill";
        s2 = "Gates";

        //Below statement will reserve 5
bytes and initialize s3 to it
        s3 = malloc(5);

        //find the length of s1 using
pointer
        while(*(s1+i))
        {
        i++;
        }
        printf ("Length of the string s1
%s is %d \n", s1,i);
```

```
        i--;
    //===================================
==========
    //reverse the string using
pointer
    while(i>=0)
    {
    *(s3+j) = *(s1+i);
    i--;
    j++;
    }
            *(s3+j) = '\0';
    printf ("Reverse of the string s3
is %s \n", s3);
    //===================================
==========
    //Copy the string s1 to s3
    i=0;
    while(*(s1+i))
    {

    *(s3+i) = *(s1+i);
    i++;
    }
    printf ("S1 copied to s3 %s \n",
s3);

    //===================================
==========
    s3 = "sgaarsalunke";
    printf ("s3 %s \n", s3);


}
```

```
C:\Users\sagar>gcc source.c

C:\Users\sagar>a
Length of the string s1 Bill is 4
Reverse of the string s3 is 11iB
S1 copied to s3 Bill
s3 sgaarsalunke
```

8.6 Dynamic memory allocation using pointers.

Arrays occupy fixed size of memory. If you declare array to store 100 integer values, total memory reserved by system is 200 bytes (100*2).

But what if we need to store only 20 integer values? At runtime, we can not resize array.

That's when dynamic memory allocation concept comes into picture. With dynamic memory mechanism, we can reserve only enough memory that is required. So we can save memory if we use dynamic memory allocation.

C provides 4 important functions that can be used to work with dynamic memory allocation.

1. malloc
2. calloc
3. realloc
4. free

Below example will clarify how to handle dynamic memory in C.

```
#include <stdio.h>
#include <stdlib.h>
int main()
{
```

```
//int * p = malloc(10*sizeof(int));
int * p = calloc(10, sizeof(int));
//both statements

if (p==NULL)
{
  printf("unable to allocate 20
bytes");
  exit(1);
 }
  int i;
for(i=0;i<10;i++)
 *(p+i) = i;
for(i=0;i<10;i++)
printf("%d ",   *(p+i) );


p = realloc(p,20*sizeof(int));
for(i=10;i<20;i++)
 *(p+i) = i;

for(i=0;i<20;i++)
printf("%d ",   *(p+i) );

free(p);

}
```

```
C:\Users\sagar>gcc source.c

C:\Users\sagar>a
0 1 2 3 4 5 6 7 8 9 0
1
2
3
4
5
6
7
8
9
```

83

9. Structures and Unions In C

9.1 Structure

So far we have used arrays to store data. But there is one drawback in arrays. We can store only data of similar type in arrays.

For example – suppose you want to store the data of employee like name, id, address etc. It is not possible to store this data in same array as data type of the id is integer and data type of name id character.

This is when structures come into picture.

In below image, we have a structure to store data for ID and Name. Total memory required by below structure is 8 bytes.

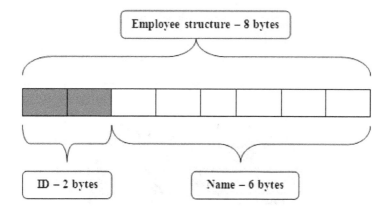

```
struct employee
{
int no;
```

```
char name[10];
int mob;
char Address[50];
}
```

Simple structure example

```
#include<stdio.h>

void main()
{
   struct dept        //declaring structure
   {
     int id;
     char name[15];
   };
     struct dept d={01,"Production"};
//Initializing structure elements
     printf("\n id=%d",d.id);
     printf("\n name=%s",d.name);
   getchar();
}
```

```
C:\Users\sagar>gcc source.c
C:\Users\sagar>a
  id=1
  name=Production
```

Array of structure

C Structure is collection of different data types (variables) which are grouped together. Whereas, array of structures

85

is nothing but collection of structures. This is also called as structure array in C.

```c
#include<stdio.h>
void main()
{
    struct dept
    {
        int id;
        char name[15];
    }stru[3];

    int i=0;
    for(i=0;i<=2;i++)
    {
        printf("\n Enter id :" );
        scanf("%d",&stru[i].id);
        printf("\n Enter name:");
        scanf("%s",stru[i].name);
    }
    for(i=0;i<=2;i++)
    {
        printf("\n id=%d name=%s", stru
[i].id, stru [i].name);
    }
getchar();
}
```

```
C:\Users\sagar>gcc source.c

C:\Users\sagar>a

 Enter id :2

 Enter name:sara

 Enter id :3

 Enter name:rana

 Enter id :4

 Enter name:sayan

 id=2 name=sara
 id=3 name=rana
 id=4 name=sayan
```

Nested structure

Nested structure in C is nothing but structure within structure. One structure can be declared inside other structure as we declare structure members inside a structure. The structure variables can be a normal structure variable or a pointer variable to access the data. You can learn below concepts in this section.

- Structure within structure in C using normal variable

- Structure within structure in C using pointer variable

Structure within structure using normal variable

```
#include<stdio.h>


struct Department
{
    int dept_id;
```

```
      char dept_name[50];
};

struct Employee
{
      int id;
      char name[20];
      float sal;
      // structure within structure
      struct Department dept;
}emp;

void main()
{
      struct Employee emp =
{12,"Sagar",15000,53,"Testing"};

printf("Department Id is:%d \n"
,emp.dept.dept_id);
printf("Department Name is:%s
\n",emp.dept.dept_name);
 printf(" Id is: %d \n", emp.id);
 printf(" Name is: %s \n", emp.name);
 printf(" Salary is: %f \n\n", emp.sal);

 getchar();
}
```

```
C:\Users\sagar>gcc source.c

C:\Users\sagar>a
Department Id is:53
Department Name is:Testing
 Id is: 12
 Name is: Sagar
 Salary is: 15000.000000
```

Structure within structure using pointer variable

```c
#include<stdio.h>


struct Department
{
    int dept_id;
    char dept_name[50];
};

struct Employee
{
    int id;
    char name[20];
    float sal;
    // structure within structure
    struct Department dept;
}emp,*empptr;

void main()
{
    struct Employee emp =
{12,"Sagar",15000,53,"Testing"};
    empptr=&emp;

  printf(" Department Id is: %d
\n",empptr->dept.dept_id);
  printf(" Department Name is: %s
\n",empptr->dept.dept_name);

  printf(" Id is: %d \n", empptr->id);
  printf(" Name is: %s \n",empptr->
name);
  printf(" Salary is: %f \n\n",empptr->
sal);


    getchar();
}
```

```
C:\Users\sagar>gcc source.c

C:\Users\sagar>a
 Department Id is: 53
 Department Name is: Testing
 Id is: 12
 Name is: Sagar
 Salary is: 15000.000000
```

9.2 Unions In C

Structure occupies the memory size that is equal to the sum of sizes of all members of the structure.

But Union occupies the memory size that is equal to the size of the largest member of the Union.

As shown in below image, total memory occupied by employee union is 6 bytes. If it was structure, memory occupied would have been 8 bytes.

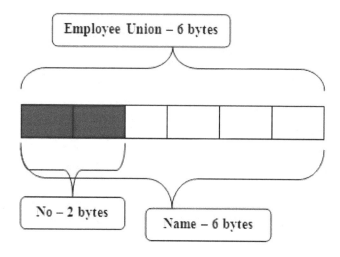

Example –

Below structure will occupy 52 bytes. But if it was union, it would have occupied 50 bytes.

```c
struct Department
{
    int dept_id;
    char dept_name[50];
};
```

```c
#include<stdio.h>
#include<string.h>

union u
{
    int a;
    float b;
    char  s1[17];
};

int main( )
{
    union u u;
    system("cls");
    u.a = 8;
    printf( "u.a : %d\n", u.a);

    u.b = 99.0;
    printf( "u.b : %f\n", u.b);

    strcpy( u.s1, "fortitude");
    printf( "u.s1 : %s\n", u.s1);
    getchar();
```

```
}
```

when execute the program after that display the below
result.

```
u.a  :  8
u.b  :  99.000000
u.s1  :  fortitude
```

10. Files In C

In c there are two types of files.

1. Text files
2. Binary files

Text files store human readable characters while binary files store machine readable characters.

10.1 Creating a text file

```
#include<stdio.h>
#include<string.h>
main( )
{
    FILE *f;
    char s1[25];
    int i;
    f = fopen("abc.txt","w");
    /* open for writing ..second
parameter specifies the mode. */
    strcpy(s1,"This is an example
line.");

    for (i = 1; i <= 10; i++)
        fprintf(f,"%s Line number %d\n",
s1, i);
    fclose(f); /* close the file before
ending program */
}
```

10.2 Reading File

Below program shows how to read the file character by character.

```
#include<stdio.h>

#include<stdlib.h>

void main()
{
    // here declare a file in pointer.
    FILE *filep;

    char ch;

    //fopen function is used to open a
text file
    //Please note that mode of the file
is r.

    filep =fopen("c:\\abc.txt","r");

    if (!filep)
    {
        printf ("File does not exist\n");
        getchar();
        exit(0);
    }

    printf("The data in file is :- \n");

    //fgetc function is used to read
the character from file.
    //fgets function is used to read
the string from a file.

    while((ch=fgetc(filep))!=EOF)
```

```
    {
      printf("%c",ch);
    }

    fclose(filep);

    // Here close the text file.

  getchar();
}
```

```
C:\Users\sagar>gcc source.c

C:\Users\sagar>a
The data in file is :-
Apple
Mango,Banana
green,red Yellow,white
Elephant,Dog
```

Below program shows how to read file line by line.

```
#include<stdio.h>
#include<stdlib.h>

void main()
{
   // here declare a file in pointer.
   FILE *filep;
   char *str = malloc(255);

   char ch;

   //fopen function is used to open a
text file
   //Please note that mode of the file
is r.
```

```
      filep =fopen("abc.txt","r");

      if (!filep)
      {
         printf ("File does not exist\n");
         getchar();
         exit(0);
      }

      printf("The data in file is :- \n");

         //fgetc function is used to read
   the character from file.
         //fgets function is used to read
   the string from a file.

      while(fgets(str,255,filep))

         {
            printf("%s",str);
         }

         fclose(filep);
   }
```

```
C:\Users\sagar>gcc source.c

C:\Users\sagar>a
The data in file is :-
Apple
Mango,Banana
green,red Yellow,white
Elephant,Dog
```

10.3 Check if file exists in C.

Below program shows how to check if file exists or not.

```
#include<stdio.h>
```

```
#include<stdlib.h>

void main()
{
    // here declare a file in pointer.
    FILE *filep;

    // try to open a text file at
location c:\abc.txt.

    //if file exists, fopen will
return not null pointer
    filep =fopen("c:\\abc.txt","r");

    if (!filep)
    {
      printf ("File does not exist\n");
      getchar();
    }
    else
    {
      printf("File exists at given
location");
    }
}
```

```
C:\Users\sagar>gcc source.c

C:\Users\sagar>a
File does not exist
```

10.4 Deleting File

We can delete the file using remove method.

```
#include<stdio.h>

void main()
```

```
{
    int ret;

    // remove method accepts the name
of file to be deleted as a parameter
    ret=remove("c:\\abc.txt");

  if(ret==0)
    {
    printf("File is deleted \n");
    }
  else
    {
    printf("File not deleted \n");
    }

getchar();

}
```

```
C:\Users\sagar>gcc source.c

C:\Users\sagar>a
File is deleted
```

10.4 Appending Files

To append contents to the file, you will have to open the file in append mode.

```c
#include <stdio.h>
#include <string.h>
main( )
{
    FILE *f;
    char s1[25];
    int i;
    f = fopen("abc.txt","a");
    /* open for writing */
```

```
    strcpy(s1,"This is an example
line.");

    for (i = 11; i <= 20; i++)
      fprintf(f,"%s Line number %d\n",
s1, i);
    fclose(f); /* close the file before
ending program */
}
```

11. Advanced topics in C

11.1 Pre-processor Directives
The C Pre processor or cpp is the macro pre-processor.

We can do below tasks using pre-processor directives.

1. Including header files
2. Expanding macro
3. Conditional compilation
4. Defining global constants.

Some examples of CPP directives are given below.

1. #include<stdio.h> - This directive tells the CPP to include contents of stdio.h file into current c source file.
2. #define PI 3.14 – This directive defines the constants.

We can also have directives that can be used for the conditional compilation.

```
#include <stdio.h>
#include <stdlib.h>

#define PI 3.14
int main()
{

#if (defined PI)
  printf(" PI is defined");
#endif
```

```
}
```

```
C:\Users\sagar>gcc source.c

C:\Users\sagar>a
 PI is defined
```

11.2 User defined Header files

We know that built-in header files contain the prototypes for many useful functions. We can also create our own header file with custom function.

For example – Let us create one header file called sum.h which contains the function sum. This function will return the sum of 2 arguments that we pass.

Source code of Sum.h header file is given below.

```
int sum(int a, int b)
{
return (a+b);
}
```

Source code of abc.c is given below. Please note how we have included above header file in abc.c and we have called sum function which is defined in sum.h

```
#include <stdio.h>
#include "sum.h"
int main()
{
printf("%d", sum(3,4));
```

```
}
```

```
C:\Users\sagar>gcc source.c
C:\Users\sagar>a
12
```

11.3 Error handling

In C we can handle errors using special variable called
errno which is defined in <errno.h> header file. Whenever
any error occurs during execution of the c program, the
error number is stored in errno variable. To print the error
description, we use below function call.

strerror(errno);

We can clear error number using below line.

Errno = 0;

```
#include <stdio.h>
#include <errno.h>
#include <string.h>
extern int errno ;
int main ()
{
    FILE * pf;
    pf = fopen ("abdc.txt", "r");

    if (pf == NULL)
    {
        printf("errno contains value :
%d\n", errno);
        printf("Human readable error
description : %s\n", strerror( errno ));
    }
    else
```

```
     {
          fclose (pf);
     }
     return 0;
}
```

```
C:\Users\sagar>gcc source.c

C:\Users\sagar>a
errno contains value : 2
Human readable error description : No such file or directory
```

11.4 Command line arguments

Command line arguments can be used to pass the input to the C program through command line.

Below screen shot shows how to execute the program with command line arguments using gcc in windows system.

We have sent one argument to the program – "sagar Salunke".

Program prints the length of the argument that we have passed.

```c
#include <stdio.h>
#include <string.h>

int main (int c, char *arg[])
{

if (c < 2)
{
        printf("too less arguments");
        return -1;
```

```
}
 printf("Number of command line
arguments - %d \n" , c);
 printf("Length of the argument is %d",
strlen(arg[1]));

}
```

```
C:\Users\sagar>gcc arg.c

C:\Users\sagar>a sagarsalunke
Number of command line arguments - 2
Length of the argument is 12
```

www.ingramcontent.com/pod-product-compliance
Lightning Source LLC
Chambersburg PA
CBHW060942050326
40689CB00012B/2550